Nikos Kazantzakis

by

PETER BIEN

 **Columbia University Press**

NEW YORK & LONDON 1972

PETER BIEN
is Professor of English at Dartmouth College.
He is the author of *L.P. Hartley, Kazantzakis and
the Linguistic Revolution in Greek Literature,* and,
in this series, *Constantine Cavafy.* He has also written
a textbook for the instruction of demotic Greek
(in collaboration with John Rassias and Chrysanthi Bien), and is
the translator of Kazantzakis' *The Last Temptation,
Saint Francis,* and *Report to Greco.*

Copyright © 1972 Columbia University Press
ISBN: 0-231-03532-2
Library of Congress Catalog Card Number: 79-186642
Printed in the United States of America

Nikos Kazantzakis

The career and reputation of Nikos Kazantzakis are both very curious. After struggling for forty years, he suddenly became an international celebrity in the early 1950s. Since then, his books have continued to appeal to a large number of cultivated readers while being generally ignored in "critical and academic circles." There is no agreement whatsoever about his ultimate worth, and it would seem impossible to predict at this stage whether he will be read fifty years after his death, like Cavafy, or will share the fate of his friend Panait Istrati, who enjoyed an immense vogue in the twenties and is now almost completely forgotten. Book reviewers and critics have tended toward polarized excesses of praise or vilification when writing about Kazantzakis. In England, for example, his novels have been called "among the most impressive of our time" and his *Odyssey* an "astonishing . . . creation," but he has also been dismissed as "an atrocious writer . . . whose faults are so glaring as to be dazzling." In Greece, many of his compatriots insist that he falsifies everything Hellenic, while some see in him the very epitome of his nation. The polarities have become so fixed that it would seem useless to argue any longer along such lines, or even to worry whether Kazantzakis is a great or an atrocious writer. Instead, let us start with the simple fact of his popularity. We may assume, since his books are terrifyingly intellectual and have no salacious interest, that his readership consists of discriminating people of superior education. No one really knows what gives certain writers a wide appeal. Perhaps it is an equal remoteness from the banal and the eccentric, perhaps just a

[3]

vague affinity between the author's concerns and those of his readers. In any case, the simple fact that Kazantzakis is interesting to many readers offers a place to begin, for the most immediate critical question then becomes: Why is he interesting, why does he speak to our condition?

I shall try to answer this question, though in a roundabout way. Kazantzakis' chief interest, I believe, lies in his totality. This of course shines through individual works, yet it is often difficult to detect until we know the career as a whole. It is a complicated and slippery totality, a visible exterior with an invisible bull inside butting against the walls. Outwardly, there is an artistic personality, a professionalism, and an elaborate world-view. Inside this three-ply integument are strains and growths—in particular, toward prose and the prosaic, toward rootedness, toward aestheticism—which challenge the outward aspect but never quite crack it. But these too, of course, are part of the whole, and it is precisely the tension between the two elements, between the masks Kazantzakis laboriously carved and the strains which came largely in spite of himself, that makes the totality so interesting and so touchingly human. To discover this interest we must go the roundabout way of establishing certain visible characteristics and then attempting to see the fluctuations within.

How, then, can we characterize Kazantzakis' artistic personality? If we can establish this personality with reasonable accuracy for the career as a whole we shall be less likely to expect the impossible from individual works. People complain, for example, that the novel *Zorba* is not realistic. But Kazantzakis' artistic personality prevented him from writing in the realistic mode. The critic who harps on defective realism in Kazantzakis' novels prevents us from granting those novels their own premises. Similarly, it is easy to say that Kazantzakis' plays are not theatrical because instead of dramatic interest they present long intellec-

[4]

tual declamations. But theatricality is larger than any one definition. Milton's *Comus,* with very little dramatic interest to be sure, was theatrical to its viewers; John Lyly wrote plays without plot, rounded characters, or dramatic tension, yet they were entertaining and theatrical for other reasons: pageant, language, even their "delicate evocations of profound ideas." What I am suggesting is that we try to discover the kind of writer Kazantzakis was, instead of condemning him for not being what he wasn't. A critic has claimed that "in the state of Greek writing as it was in [Kazantzakis'] youth it was hardly possible for him to see the importance of Cavafy or later of Seferis, nor was he intelligent enough . . . to overcome the obstacles and make the same discoveries about poetry and style for himself as greater writers had made." What this says, in effect, is that all significant literature in our age is terse, restrained, ironic. But Kazantzakis could never have written poetry in the style of Seferis or Seferis' model T. S. Eliot, any more than he could have written Pinteresque plays, or novels in the manner of Jane Austen. In his plays he favored the declamatory mode and elaborate *mise en scène* rather than wit or psychological subtlety. In his novels he was allegorical, rambling, polysemous, rhetorical. In everything he displayed romantic excess; he painted sprawling canvases rather than miniatures; he valued fervor over precision, sincerity over craftsmanship. These are constants in his career and should be accepted as such. They characterize certain artists in all ages and assuredly are among the multiform ways that the human spirit can validly, and beautifully, manifest itself.

But how can we sum him up? What single rubric is flexible enough to define his artistic personality? A workable one might be E. M. Forster's term "prophet," by which Forster means a writer who stimulates us not so much by realism, plotting, characterization, or a web of causal relationships as by a tone of voice, and in particular a tone which displays an urgency seen in

[5]

the Old Testament prophets. In prophetic writers, content and form are subordinate to *élan*.

Kazantzakis liked to think of himself as an Akritas stationed bravely and alone at the borders of light, apostrophizing the abyss. His circumstances, however, made him a workaday professional writer dependent on his pen for a livelihood. This professionalism is the second element of his totality that we must consider, for only by recognizing the attitudes and diversity it engendered can we avoid expecting from him what we normally expect from a novelist, poet, or playwright. He was none of these. Instead, he was a professional man-of-letters, by which I mean someone writing almost continually and willing to work in any and all forms that happen to present themselves. With the exception of the *Odyssey*, which occupied him on and off for more than a decade, he simply wrote what had to be written, quickly, and then turned with compulsive haste to the next project. Too busy to retreat into genre-specialization, he produced an *œuvre* of astonishing variety. Besides novels, poems, and plays, he did travel books, children's stories, fictionalized biographies of historical figures, literary history, encyclopedia articles on every conceivable subject, journalism, political and ethical polemics, translations in prose and verse of scientific, literary, and philosophical works, school textbooks, and even a dictionary. It is hardly surprising, given such prodigality, that he produced no single work which is fully satisfying from a technical point of view. Some of his novels, plays, and poems are very bad indeed, and the good ones are uneven. Furthermore, his best writing sometimes appears in nonliterary volumes which he himself considered secondary. I think of the splendid polemics in his occasional political effusions, and of descriptive and narrative gems scattered in the travel articles. In so many of his works where we may demur at the total effect we nevertheless find astonishing fragments: imaginative metaphors, vivid and

[6]

moving descriptions, convincing wisdom. My point is that we should avoid belaboring the fact that Kazantzakis was not a deliberate craftsman pushing back the frontiers of a given genre, and should accept him in his totality as the prodigal, professional, diverse man-of-letters that he was.

Kazantzakis' professionalism led him to subordinate letters in the narrow sense to something much more comprehensive. Another man-of-letters, G. K. Chesterton, once said: "I have never taken my books seriously; but I take my opinions quite seriously." Kazantzakis did take some of his books seriously, but this was chiefly because they promulgated his opinions. For him, being a man-of-letters meant being a controversialist promulgating and defending his ideas. This in turn meant—in the largest sense—being an intellectual. Kazantzakis' true profession was that of thinking and articulating, of entering his quite extraordinary brain in the lists against what he considered obscurantism and outmoded thought. Writing was only one tool among many, but the one which he found served him best. (He gradually learned that as a speechmaker and political organizer he was much less effective.) To be a man-of-letters, furthermore, meant assuming a life-style consistent with one's opinions, and remembering that a play or novel was just one aspect of a total response.

We must pass now to the third and most important element in Kazantzakis' outward integument, his ideas. The first thing to realize about them is that they dictated his life-style as a man-of-letters and accounted for his fervor as a prophet. Though severely intellectual, they were not bloodless; they had for him the urgency and passion of emotions. The next thing to realize is their constancy. Despite Kazantzakis' growth in many areas during the five decades of his career, he adhered throughout to certain very basic positions developed at the start. There is no mistaking what these positions were, for Kazantzakis supple-

[7]

mented his imaginative writings with didactic glosses lest his readers misunderstand. As we shall see, he began with a theory of history and then expanded this to a theory of metahistory. The keystone of his historical thinking may be called his "doctrine of the transitional age." The trouble with our times, Kazantzakis argued, is that we are caught in the middle. On the one hand we have lost our spontaneous appreciation of this world's beauty; on the other we have lost our faith in the heavens above. We cannot be pagans because Christianity has poisoned our attitude toward material things; we cannot be Christians because Darwinism has destroyed the perfect spiritual world which is the necessary basis of Christian behavior. We are thus the melancholy victims of a transitional age. The novella *Snake and Lily* (1906) treats in particular the impossibility of an idealized, pagan devotion to earthly beauty. Things have come to such a pass that the heroine must choose suicide rather than existence in a contingent world. The novella's complement, a remarkable one-act play published slightly later (1909) and sardonically entitled *Comedy,* focuses on the impossibility of Christian hope. Taken together, these works show the deaths of both Apollo and Christ, deaths which in effect proclaim "no exit" for those with spiritual aspiration. An early novel bearing the significant title *Broken Souls* presents additional victims.

As Kazantzakis advanced in his career and broadened his own experience, he merely put old wine in new bottles. The doctrine of the transitional age remained; the historical details changed. But although his characters continued to be squashed in the jaws of conflicting impossibilities, he refused to let them remain broken souls. In the play *Day Is Breaking* (produced 1907) the theories are developed in a semi-optimistic way and an exit of sorts is provided. Lalo, the tragic heroine, is trapped once more between Christ (duty) and Apollo (beauty, romantic love). But now a third god is introduced as well: Dionysus. His spokesman, a forceful polemicist resembling Kazantzakis himself, preaches a virile neo-paganism which will overthrow both Christian self-denial and romantic self-indulgence. Lalo knows that this third way is right, but she does not have the strength to follow it because she is caught in a transitional age. A broken soul, she finds her only solution in suicide. Yet the play is optimistic in a qualified way, the implication being that in our minds, our imaginations, we can escape the trap. The transitional age has advanced to the point where we can envision the succeeding age and herald it, even if we cannot bring our outward lives into full accord with our vision. Right thought is possible, right action is not. Moreover, the very proclamation of right thought — what Kazantzakis was later to term the "Cry"—will help to make right action possible. If day is breaking, full daylight cannot be far behind.

The increasing optimism of these early works tempted Kazantzakis, but he yielded only once to the next logical stage. In his play *The Masterbuilder* (1909) the dauntless hero bludgeons his way to freedom in act as well as thought. The play mirrors the political optimism Kazantzakis shared with other Greeks at the time, but it contradicts his earlier equation of freedom with complete immateriality and thus with death, as well as his romantic sense that fulfillment must involve the infinite. In addition, Kazantzakis had already given the doctrine of the transitional age a cosmological as well as a historical dimension, seeing the universe itself as a huge transition between two abysses. All his subsequent work is a struggle to devise some kind of exit from these metahistorical jaws without giving way either to the facile optimism of *The Masterbuilder* or the resignation of *Snake and Lily* and *Comedy.* One result is Kazantzakis' well-known "heroic pessimism." We find hero after hero caught in a transitional situation, able to envision

[9]

the exit imaginatively and therefore to voice a Cry, but confined to only two kinds of action. The first of these is suicide once more. Now, however, self-destruction is no longer a defect of will, a capitulation by a broken soul before the superior forces of history and fate. On the contrary, it can be a supremely voluntaristic act, the ultimate affirmation of strength, and one which pushes the universe forward both historically and cosmologically. Though a formula, this solution allowed Kazantzakis sufficient scope because he could vary the historical circumstances and also the vibrancy with which his characters responded. In *Nikephoros Phokas* and *Julian the Apostate,* for example, the heroes are still in great danger of being crushed; in *Christ Recrucified, Captain Michael, The Last Temptation, Kapodistrias,* and *Melissa,* their strength is much more assured. The relative success of each work artistically depends on how well it fuses history with cosmology, the particular transition with the general, and how completely it makes us forget that both characterization and plot are formulaic.

A second solution which Kazantzakis allowed was art. In his search for an exit he came to insist that the Cry itself could be an affirmative action. Some achieved freedom and cheated fate by heroic suicide, others by heroic assertions of the imagination. But he tended not to broadcast this solution in his works, perhaps because it was the one he adopted in his life. It is explicit enough, however, in *Zorba, Buddha,* and parts of the *Odyssey;* it is crucially implicit, as I hope to show, in the late novels. This solution answered to a natural aestheticism in Kazantzakis which he could not suppress, but it also emerged inevitably from the cosmological expansions he gave his original ideas, and in particular from his conviction that the universe itself is evolving toward self-consciousness.

But to understand how Kazantzakis developed his earliest ideas into the formulaic solutions I have just tried to sketch, we must dwell upon his time of philosophical inquiry in Paris (October, 1907–February, 1909). His purpose there was to broaden his understanding of history until he could discern his own role in the cosmic process. The deliberate nature of his attempt at self-consciousness is indicated in a letter he wrote at the time: "I want to work out an individual, personal conception of life," he said, "a world-theory and a theory of man's destiny, and then, in accord with these, systematically and with a determined purpose and program, to write what I shall write." He accordingly immersed himself in modern philosophical doctrine, in epistemology and metaphysics especially, with particular emphasis on Kant. This in turn led him to the pair of figures who were to have such a lasting effect on his thought — Nietzsche and Bergson.

Much has been said, and quite rightly, about Kazantzakis' debt to Nietzsche, very little about his debt to Bergson. Yet it is clear that, of the two, Bergson played a much greater role in Kazantzakis' intellectual life, enabling him to expand the doctrine of the transitional age into a complete cosmology and giving him a new vocabulary ("ascent," "transubstantiation," *élan,* etc.) with which to articulate his system. Kazantzakis' attraction to Nietzsche was chiefly emotional. Whereas Bergson was cold and scientific, Nietzsche embodied a life-style, an artistic personality which Kazantzakis dreamed of emulating. He too wanted to be a prophetic tempest churning together philosophy, art, and moral fervor until ideas became incandescent. He liked the way Nietzsche's writings spilled out into ecstasy, the way "the sperm rose to his head." And he did not care if the Master's ideas lacked originality; his importance was that he converted these ideas into passions.

Nietzsche's main contribution to Kazantzakis' thought-system was his insistence that nihilism need not be a symptom of decadence, that it might be instead a positive force, a homeopathic

[11]

medicine to hasten the end of the nihilistic impasse characterizing our own transitional age. The influence was thus largely negative. He taught Kazantzakis that to smash old values is a moral imperative if we wish new ones to emerge, daybreak to develop into full day. In particular, he taught him to reject Christianity, since hopes and fears based on a false conception of the universe can only lead to decreased moral vitality. The whole value-system resting on the mistaken notion of a rational universe had to be smashed. Nietzsche thus encouraged in Kazantzakis an antipathy toward everything bourgeois, which meant everything comfortable, inert, rational, equitable, and flabby. This hatred embraced democracy, cosmopolitanism, socialism, egalitarianism, pacifism, tolerance, woman's rights, rationalism—everything liberal, everything which attempts to minimize pain, conflict, or other vital manifestations of the flux, unrest, contradiction, irrationality, and self-overcoming which Nietzsche posited as the true nature of reality. In sum, Nietzsche's negative teachings encouraged Kazantzakis to smash a false metaphysic and the false religion, morality, and social organization based on that metaphysic.

Perhaps Nietzsche's greatest effect was to prepare Kazantzakis for Bergson. He did this because he insisted that our value-system must accord with scientific knowledge. Ever since Kazantzakis saw his allegiance to the Christian world-view destroyed by Darwinism, he had nevertheless clung to a belief in spirit, infinitude, and salvation while knowing that these had to be redefined in modern, scientific terms. Here now was Bergson with redefinitions ready-to-hand and with a "proof" that the central, driving force in the universe is an evolving vitality which transubstantiates flesh into spirit. Kazantzakis was naturally eager to listen, and thrice-eager to use this as a hardheaded intellectual foundation for the spiritual yearnings he had developed earlier. Christ had killed off Apollo, Darwin had killed off Christ. Dionysus was unscientific and nonevolutionary. Bergson now provided Kazantzakis with a new, "true" god.

To discover the nature of this god we must first ask ourselves certain cosmological questions, precisely those which Kazantzakis asked and answered under Bergson's guidance. They are the "where" questions: Where have we come from, where are we going? The answers are given succinctly in the Prologue to Kazantzakis' *Spiritual Exercises,* the book in which he eventually expounded his Bergsonian ideas with Nietzschean passion. "We come from a dark abyss," Kazantzakis states there, and "we end in a dark abyss." Life thus becomes a "luminous interval" between two black voids. These formulations of course support Kazantzakis' earlier doctrine of the transitional age. Indeed they expand it into a cosmological principle. The whole of life, the whole of the cosmos, is now a transition from one void to another.

The next question involves the relation of the luminous interval to the abysses at either end. These might seem to annihilate and negate life, rendering all evolution futile. Bergson taught Kazantzakis, however, that this is not the case. The so-called voids at either end of life are absolute freedom, absolute spirituality, and are therefore—paradoxically—the fulfillment of life's strivings rather than their negation.

The Bergsonian "proof" of this is long and complicated, but we must examine at least some of the ingredients if we wish to understand Kazantzakis' concept of god. Bergson posits a preexistent life force (*élan vital*), a pure energy which wills to become alive. But to become alive it must collaborate with matter. Not that matter is anything separate from the force; life, Bergson writes, is the vital current "loaded with matter, that is, with congealed parts of its own substance." However, once the life force has created life, it tends to divest itself of its congealments and return to pure energy. Evolution shows us that life is a creative action which unmakes itself. It is change which moves toward inertness, heterogeneity which moves toward homogeneity. Our solar system, says Bergson, is "ever exhausting something of the mutability it contains." In other words, death is not something that negates all the "desires" of the cosmos, but rather something toward which the cosmos itself, life itself, is moving. The black abyss at the end of life is not a sudden, arbitrary, "unjust" negation of life; it is the ineluctable, logical conclusion of the very process it seems to nullify. Death, in effect, is life burning itself out; both life and death are willed by the same "god." Furthermore, the sloughing off of matter means a release of the primal force, a complete freeing and spiritualizing of what had previously been weighed down by its own congealments. Life evolves toward increasing spiritualization by means of transubstantiation. Rocks evolve to plants, then to animals, then to man; sensation develops into instinct, then intelligence, and finally self-consciousness. But life's crown in this regard is death, when all materiality is dissolved. Annihilation equals fulfillment.

We have reached the point now where we can begin to discuss the new, "true" god which Kazantzakis found with Bergson's help. To do this, however, we must first realize that although Bergson strives for a monism, he finds it easier to speak of spirit and matter as two distinct and antagonistic entities. Thus he pictures (1) the life force surging upward toward creativity, motion, heterogeneity, consciousness, and (2) matter pressing downward toward stability and homogeneity. Life is the meeting of the two. Kazantzakis echoes this in the Prologue to *Spiritual Exercises:* "In the temporary living organism, these two streams collide: (a) the ascent toward composition, toward life, toward immortality; (b) the descent toward decomposition, toward matter, toward death. Both streams well up from the depths of

[14]

primordial essence." The Prologue goes on to state that "it is our duty . . . to grasp that vision which can embrace and harmonize these two . . . indestructible forces." Here precisely, in this synthesizing vision, Kazantzakis found his new god. Seen monistically, god is the entire evolutionary process; he is the primordial essence which wills first its own congealment into life and then the unmaking of this creative action. But the human mind can apprehend this synthesis only in rare intuitive moments, and thus tends to fall into dualistic and analytical formulations. Just as Bergson speaks of matter and spirit as distinct entities, so Kazantzakis analyzes his god into distinct and indeed antagonistic "persons" (hypostases). One of these corresponds to Bergson's downward stream and another to Bergson's upward stream. The latter is further analyzed into two aspects, sexual and mental, so that in sum we have one-in-three, a trihypostatic monad!

The descending god is everything that frustrates the life force's upward surge. It is Necessity, the inexorable downward push of matter toward decomposition. In the *Odyssey* this god is called the "killer"; he is heroically but always unsuccessfully defied by man, and in particular by man's sexual and mental powers. Indeed, man's purpose in life (seen narrowly in terms of this god only) is to kill the killer-god in all his manifestations — that is, to battle against all forms of stagnation, homogeneity, and inertness.

The god corresponding to Bergson's upward movement is much more complicated. I have indicated that he is further analyzed into two aspects, the sexual and the mental, but this too is misleading, for these seemingly antagonistic hypostases have much in common.

Seen in his totality, the upward-surging god is also a killer, but a killer with a difference. "Ce qui dévore l'homme, je l'appelle Dieu," Kazantzakis wrote in a letter, at the same time

[15]

proclaiming his love for this god and his hope that he would never cease to be devoured. This, then, is not the downward-moving god I spoke of earlier, for man's response in that case is defiance and hate. Here, Kazantzakis is invoking the primordial force which drives man to burn himself out in the interests of pushing life upward. This god is the Cry rolling down from Sinai: Reach what you cannot! Evolve!

But the self-incineration needed if one is to respond fully to this Cry can take both sexual and mental forms. Sexually, man burns himself out in order to evolve by means of progeny. The over-all upward surge is accomplished only because each generation produces vibrant successors and then dies. If we truly understand this god who devours man, we will love him for the opportunity he gives us to participate in the universal process which demands our own extinction. In the *Spiritual Exercises,* Kazantzakis speaks of this god as the husband. His wife is matter. He is the sperm inside all the eggs of the universe, the male propulsion of the upward stream working inside the female inertia of the downward stream. (This metaphysical or rather metabiological view of women is of course reflected in all of Kazantzakis' works.) He is the force that loves all things and sticks to none, loves all things *because* he sticks to none; for only through successive deaths can he jump from body to body and stake out the red line which is life. This god is the spark, the flame centered in man's loins.

The same god in his other aspect pushes man to burn himself out mentally. Here, too, the metaphor of flame is appropriate. In the *Odyssey* Kazantzakis speaks of the mind as a hearth containing a world-destroying world-creating spark. Or we might say, as Kazantzakis liked to, that the sperm can also reside in the head. God in this aspect is the upward-surging force pushing all of created life toward self-consciousness. This recalls Bergson's view that consciousness is the opposite of materiality and

[16]

We should burn ourselves out in the service of something beyond ourselves, and thus transubstantiate our flesh into spirit. The greatest sin becomes satisfaction, an immobility making evolution stand still and smothering god. Vitality, the life force strutting in full regalia, is the greatest virtue. All actions arising sincerely and intensely from man's vital center are good, for such actions imitate the gushing *élan* of which we are part. Conversely, all actions or thoughts which bring completion, which close off further development and therefore serve the forces of stagnation and inertia, are bad.

But these prescriptions were still too general and abstract. Kazantzakis knew that he had to pursue the elusive problem of individual response until he could pin it to the here and now. Yet he also knew that to provide a precise formula for "vital, creative action" would be a contradiction in terms, since such action by definition must be nonformulaic. To escape this dilemma Kazantzakis had recourse to his old favorite, the doctrine of the transitional age. The ways of saving god are many, he said. In various ages men as diverse as Jesus, Jenghiz Khan, Shakespeare, Lenin, El Greco, Zorba, Buddha, Psycharis (the "Saint George" who killed the dragon of puristic Greek), Don Quixote, Nietzsche, and Dante have been saviors of god, each in his own manner. But not all paths are applicable in any given era. For each transitional age there is a dominant way to fight stagnation and to liberate the flame. There is also a dominant group which follows this way. Kazantzakis' nonformulaic formula, therefore, is that we must seek out the group in our own age which seems to have the greatest vitality and sincerity, the group whose actions favor motion, creativity, freedom, and tend to open new possiblities rather than bring completion. In his own age, he concluded, the way chosen by the ascending spirit was war. The groups he admired at various stages in his life were militant ones which did not shrink from violence as a

[19]

means of expressing their vitality. Kazantzakis by no means loved violence for its own sake. What he loved was his god, the life force evolving toward spirituality by devouring man, and it is only because of his conviction that warfare was the twentieth century's strongest force for spiritual growth that he lent it his support. I state this in order to emphasize how absolutely central his world-view was to all his writings and proclamations. To understand any individual work we must see it in light of what was constant in all the works. This will save us from misinterpreting his enthusiasms and forcing upon him narrow allegiances which completely misrepresent the facts. If we forget the metaphysical constants we can easily make the mistake of thinking him a communist (he admired Lenin) or a fascist (he admired Mussolini). Conversely, when we read a book like *The Last Temptation* we might mistakenly believe that in his dotage he renounced violence for Christian love. The truth is that he was neither a communist, fascist, nor Christian; he was a Bergsonist. If at various stages in his life he admired militant Greek nationalists, Lenin, Mussolini, African blacks, and Mao, it was because these people had discerned, so he thought, the particular spiritual path appropriate for our age. If he presented Christ as a hero it was not because he himself had reverted to Christianity, but rather because he admired Christ as a savior of god following a way appropriate to another transitional situation. Once he had discovered his Bergsonian god, he maintained his allegiance with a diabolical consistency; indeed his sin (for those who feel the need of accusing him of something) was not in the deepest sense his moments of olympian heartlessness toward individual suffering, but—strangely—his uncompromising loyalty to the spirit, a loyalty which tended to make his system such a neat response to the particular problems of our time that it called a halt, cutting him off from further progress and negating precisely what the system was meant to accomplish.

[20]

For me, however, this very sin—the fact that the great fighter against orthodoxies allowed himself to become the partial prisoner of his own orthodoxy—is precisely what makes Kazantzakis interesting and, indeed, human. Best of all, he himself realized the trap he had created, and though he never succeeded in escaping fully, his struggles against his own orthodoxy make him a man of true stature.

All the major ideas in Kazantzakis' world-view were acquired by the time he left Paris at the age of twenty-six. In the dozen years intervening before he formulated his position definitively in the *Spiritual Exercises* there were reinforcements and shifts of emphasis, but nothing substantially new. When Kazantzakis returned to Greece in 1909 and attempted to act on his beliefs, he found encouragement in the nationalistic mystique of Ion Dragoumis—itself an amalgam of Nietzsche and Barrès. This stressed Greece's vibrancy and its right to self-assertion, all, however, in a context of philosophical pessimism. When this vibrancy burned itself out in 1922 in a universal ignominy mocking Dragoumis' vision, Kazantzakis discovered himself suddenly attracted (a) to Oswald Spengler's declaration that Western civilization is in decline and (b) to Buddhism's insistence on the vanity of all human desire. Spengler was helpful because, arguing from historical "law," he predicted that the next phase would involve "a new element of inwardness." He called this a "Second Religiousness" and asserted that it would start "with Rationalism's fading out into helplessness." Though Kazantzakis called it "metacommunism" he meant more or less the same thing: a culture "where the worship of the machine, of reason and of practical goals will be considered unworthy." Spengler reinforced Kazantzakis' metabiological belief in an evolution moving beyond practical reason toward inwardness and intuitive wisdom.

But of all the influences between the Paris years and the

composition of *Spiritual Exercises,* Buddhism was the most important. In reading the Eastern scriptures in Vienna in 1922, Kazantzakis reencountered in concentrated form certain Buddhistic elements which had come into his earlier thinking indirectly, mostly via Schopenhauer. His distrust of the phenomenal world dates from *Snake and Lily.* From Bergson he learned "scientifically" that matter does not exist in its own right and that the abyss is ultimate reality. All this he found expressed starkly in the Buddhistic insistence that phenomena are a deceptive phantasmagoria of nothingness and that we should therefore purge ourselves of desire and embrace the void. It is important to note that he was attracted to this extreme and distorted form of his own ideas in a period of great personal disillusion and pessimism, a private little transitional age between an allegiance to Greek nationalism which had just died and an allegiance to Lenin which was struggling to be born. He thus listened momentarily to a temptation urging him to become a broken soul. But this path was so completely contrary to his own world-view, which taught that we reach the abyss by living to the full and burning ourselves out, that he was able to resist. Ultimately, his flirtation with this philosophy served simply to reinforce certain of his own ideas. For example, in determining how to save god in a particular transitional age he could easily have forgotten his awareness that the entire cosmos is a colossal transitional age between one abyss and another. Buddhism helped him retain this awareness.

With these adjustments behind him, Kazantzakis was ready to set down his definitive world-view, the *Spiritual Exercises.* He called his book a metacommunistic credo, which meant in effect a theology of activism, a justification for burning up the decadent remains of capitalist, bourgeois civilization in the interests not so much of economic or social justice (i.e., materialistic progress) as of a new, vital inwardness higher in the

[22]

spiritual scale than either capitalism or communism—in the interests, more precisely, of an inwardness capable of discovering and honoring the Kazantzakian world-view! For Kazantzakis, the aim of the Revolution was to raise men sufficiently in the evolutionary scale to make them understand what he himself had understood about ultimate reality. The book's ingredients are everything that we have been discussing: the two abysses, the luminous interval between, the relation of that interval to the abysses, god's trihypostatic nature, our duty to save him, how to do this in our own transitional age. But Kazantzakis is not content simply to state the conclusions of his own philosophical quest; true to his title, he also offers a systematic manual of the steps leading to enlightenment. Like Yeats, he places gyres within gyres; while one set of steps leads in a Bergsonian way from the whole circle to the precise point which is our person, another set begins with this Self and leads outward to the whole. This in turn presupposes a theory of knowledge. Kazantzakis begins, therefore, with an epistemological section called "The Preparation," which is in effect a Kantian critique of pure reason. Dividing reality into phenomena and noumena, he insists that the mind can deal only with the former, though even here it simply squeezes phenomena into its own categories: "I impose order on disorder and give a face—my face—to chaos." Epistemologically, our first duty is to recognize these limitations of the human mind. As for the essential, noumenal realm, this hopefully can be known too—not by the mind, of course, but by the heart (Bergson's "intuition"). The second duty is to attempt to pierce to this unified essence beyond appearances. Let us skip the crucial third duty for a moment, for in the psychology of spiritual questing this can only come after, not before, the next two exercises. In the first of these, "The March," Kazantzakis describes the mind's attempt to understand phenomena; in the second, "The Vision," he describes the

[23]

heart's attempt to understand noumena. The march employs the method of expanding consciousness; it is a journey through phenomena beginning with the self-centeredness of the babe and ending in the universal awareness of the sage. Though this awareness can only tell us of the *relationships* among phenomena, it can give an intimation at least of the Oneness behind the visible world. Thus it prepares us for the heart's vision, which is the next step. Psychologically, this involves an intuitive awareness which pierces through time to a sense of Bergsonian "duration," to a "momentary eternity which encloses everything, past and future." What is seen behind time and phenomena is of course the succession without distinction of Bergson's *élan vital,* of the primordial spirit struggling painfully upward via matter and transubstantiating that matter into spirit.

But now that the mind and heart have done their work, we come to the third duty. The mind, which hoped to impose order on the phenomenal realm, imposed upon it nothing but relationships derived subjectively from its own categories; the heart, which hoped to apprehend the noumenal realm, apprehended merely a human meaning, a human myth, and imposed this upon the unknowable. The third duty, therefore, is to conquer the mind's hope to understand phenomena and the heart's hope to understand noumena. We abolish these dualities in a synthetic, joyous acceptance of the meaninglessness of our existence: "Where are we going? Do not ask! . . . Life is good and death is good. . . . I surrender myself to everything. . . . It is your duty . . . to say 'Nothing exists!'"

This would seem to nullify all that has gone before, but it does not. We must realize that this final acceptance of meaninglessness, though a surpassing of the previous attempt to discover meaning, is not a rejection of that attempt. Just as in the Bergsonian system god can only achieve his goal of noncongealment by the laborious process of evolution through congealment, so

[24]

the acceptance of meaninglessness can only be achieved after a previous conviction that meaning can be found. Only when the mind and heart have labored futilely in pursuit of their respective chimeras does man have a right to proclaim universal futility. This proclamation cannot nullify the previous efforts since these are its own necessary precondition. We must remember that Kazantzakis was toiling to develop a rationale for action while remaining within a framework of philosophical pessimism. He is telling us that the mind and heart must burn themselves out through aspiration if the freedom of nonaspiration is ever to be achieved. He is telling us furthermore that this is also the "rhythm" of the universe. This obviously is not communist doctrine. It is Kazantzakis' *meta*communist credo, a justification for trying to make the world a better place not in spite of the abyss but because of it.

Thus the spiritual exercises conclude—or all but conclude—with a section on practical behavior. The third duty must be held in abeyance until we have burned ourselves out. Kazantzakis passes directly from "The Vision" to "The Action," reminding us that once we have discovered "the rhythm of God's march," our responsibililty is to adjust the rhythm of our small and fleeting lives to that larger rhythm. This section begins with a metaphysics of action, the relationship between man and god; it proceeds to a morality of action, the relationship between man and man, defining good and evil in ways we have seen. The final section insists that our actions should push nature itself forward in the evolutionary process, and reminds us that each man must do this in his own way. In the original version, Kazantzakis followed this section with a recapitulation of the third duty but then concluded positively with a call to each man to shoulder his Supreme Responsibility of saving god in the here and now. This he modified in 1928 during another personal transition, brought on this time by his disillusion with the Soviet Union.

[25]

The epilogue called "The Silence" does not add anything new; it simply lets Buddha have the last word, reminding us that the red track Kazantzakis so laboriously illumined for us does not really exist. (Cosmologically, this means that matter is just a deceptive form of energy; psychologically, that our sensual and intellectual conception of supposedly objective reality is just a projection of our mind's subjective categories.) In the revised version, therefore, the luminous interval called life is framed — as it should be — between a Prologue and Epilogue asserting the two abysses of nonexistence. Without being nullified thereby, all the efforts of the human mind, heart, and body are encased in universal vanity.

This, then, is the doctrine which remained constant throughout Kazantzakis' entire career and suffused all of his works, accounting for their prophetic urgency. This is the total response which he felt must govern his life-style as well as his books. The fruit of his intellectual engagement with society's problems, it constituted his great hope for guiding men upwards toward a better life. But it was also, strangely, a significant obstacle in his path toward artistic perfection.

I stressed at the beginning that we must see Kazantzakis in his totality. This means seeing how each work issues from an amalgam of his prophetic zeal, his professionalism, and the central doctrine just described. But once we look at the works in this way we may also become aware that the best of them strain to transcend (and paradoxically to fulfill) the doctrine, to undercut the prophetic voice to some degree, and to modify the professionalism. We begin to see flexibility in some or all of the areas which make up the outward integument of Kazantzakis' totality, a flexibility which came at first in spite of Kazantzakis himself, but which he gradually began to recognize and honor.

As I suggested earlier, his artistic task in each work was to find a particular historical situation which could be fused successfully with the general cosmological situation as he saw it. He then had to show his hero burning himself out in this context which rendered all action futile but in which, paradoxically, a freely-willed death, or a Cry, was not futile at all, since either imitated the universal rhythm and pushed evolution forward, saving god. The artistic problem, however, was to trick the reader into forgetting that all this was completely formulaic, and Kazantzakis could not do this very well until he became capable of transcending his own formulas in ways I hope to exhibit. Though he never abandoned or even cracked his external integument, he did modify it in crucial ways, the most important of which involved an aestheticizing of his world-view.

We shall be able to see this development if we look first at the *Odyssey*, the most ostentatiously "total" of all his works but also one which does not transcend formula. Then, in light of our findings, we may compare what Kazantzakis achieved later on.

The *Odyssey* is a monstrous and extraordinary poem which retells the *Spiritual Exercises* by means of picture, metaphor, character, and plot. A mythopoesis of doctrine, it continues a strong tradition in literary history. I stated earlier that we should avoid condemning Kazantzakis' works out of our own preconceptions (which probably include a prejudice against mythopoeticized doctrine) and that in measuring his achievement we should remember how much larger literature is than current fashion. Though the *Odyssey* is decidedly far from contemporary literary modes, it is near to ones practiced honorably in the past, and supremely by Dante and Milton. We should recognize its genre as a legitimate one and grant the poem its own assumptions before we begin to criticize.

The epic attempts to portray the entire cosmic situation as

[27]

understood by Bergson. Thus it presents a luminous interval surrounded by two dark abysses, and within the interval traces the life force's journey through matter in a creative process which unmakes itself, transubstantiating matter into spirit. The prologue and epilogue call our attention to the dark Silence at each end of existence. The sun rises at the beginning, inaugurating life, sets at the end, extinguishing it. Multiple levels are established immediately, for the sun is also Odysseus' (i.e., man's) mind. Thus the luminous interval consists of unreal shadows produced by our subjective categories. When the entire universe disintegrates into nothingness at the conclusion, it is because Odysseus' mind has gone dark.

The epic proper is divided into twenty-four books which are the alpha to omega of existence. But integrated into this universal history are the additional levels of contemporary politics and personal vicissitude. Politically, the epic uses our own transitional age as the hidden setting for Odysseus' efforts to save god. This means that violence is the hero's initial way of transubstantiating matter into spirit; it means, furthermore, that Odysseus destroys decadent establishments (the bourgeois West) in the interests of blond barbarians (the Russians). But Odysseus is not a communist, and although he cooperates with figures standing loosely for Lenin, Trotsky, Stalin, and Rosa Luxemburg, he ultimately leaves them and their narrowness behind in order to continue on his metacommunistic quest for a new inwardness.

On the level of personal vicissitude the epic reflects Kazantzakis' frustrations. He tried, for example, to convince the Russians to overcome their materialism (their ideals were just Americanism in disguise, he told them) and to move toward the inwardness of metacommunism. But, too mystical for the Stalinists and too pessimistic for the Trotskyites, he was ignored by everyone. All this is confessed with remarkable frankness in the loosely autobiographical novel *Toda Raba,* written hastily in 1929 immediately after the frustration it records and immediately before the *Odyssey's* crucial second draft. Kazantzakis' alter ego in the novel fails not only in politics but in love and friendship. In the epic, by contrast, the hero is a great activist, a remarkable lover, and an irresistible friend. Seen on this (admittedly secondary) level, the *Odyssey* is a wish-fulfilling fantasy reflecting Kazantzakis' problems by means of inversion.

But the poem's cosmic level is by far the most important, the one into which everything else is integrated. It is Bergsonian—that is to say, incomprehensible if we ignore Kazantzakis' metabiological beliefs. I have already spoken of the cosmic frame encasing the alpha to omega of existence. Experience, both bodily and mental, is compassed by universal vanity, and the epic explores this total situation in an attempt to show (1) that death is not life's negation but its fulfillment, (2) that life on earth, despite all its struggles which seem to result only in failure, is necessary and good. Why is it good? Because only through fleshly experience can we evolve to the understanding that all fleshly experience is futile. Why is it necessary? Because this is the way the universe operates. Do not ask further!

The twenty-four books fill in the details. Odysseus, in whom all men and all history are represented, adjusts his life superbly to the universal rhythm; he imitates god, saving both god and himself in the process. This imitation naturally takes the form of an evolution from brutishness to refinement, sexuality to intellectuality, martial exploit to imaginative exploit; from instinctive responses to deliberative ones, and thence to a self-conscious playing with the shadows which we mistakenly think are real. In these and all the other ways that he evolves, Odysseus is of course defying satisfaction and stagnation in the interests of motion, freedom, and decongealment. In the largest sense he moves from the outwardness of destroying, copulating, and building to an inwardness in which all his outward actions

[29]

are recapitulated on the level of the imagination. He burns himself out twice over, loves all things and sticks to none twice over, as though operating first in the lower half and then in the upper of a multileveled Byzantine icon. These two realms correspond roughly to the two halves of the epic, with the City acting as fulcrum. Odysseus first evolves to the point where he knows what actions are demanded of him. After burning up civilization, he rebuilds it. When his great creation is obliterated by a life force that loves all things yet sticks to none, he is then able to evolve to the third duty whereby he joyously accepts the futility of action and the meaninglessness of existence. On this upper level of the icon he learns to say "Nothing exists" in various ways, and moves steadily toward the eternal Silence which is his essence and fulfillment.

We must remember that Odysseus is not only imitating the universe, he is saving it, enabling it to evolve. The life force can liberate itself only through the successively refined congealments of Odysseus' (mankind's) upward march. This universal evolution is indicated by the series of divine masks corresponding to Odysseus' expanding awareness as (negatively) he defies the killer god by warring against all forms of stagnation, first with his martial and sexual lances, then with his mind, and as (positively) he serves the upward-moving god by burning himself out in the creation of progeny, of societies, and finally of complete self-consciousness, the most spiritual aspect of the trihypostatic monad. The masks become increasingly less bestial as the divine flame is gradually liberated from its prison of flesh, until the final face has no features at all—"for all its flesh had turned to soul, and soul to air!" Thus god himself is vaporized back into his initial purity. With Odysseus' death—the death of the Mind which has enabled life's shadows to dance before us as though they were real—all that remains of the universe is a voiceless wail lingering like incandescence from a disintegrated star, a nostalgia for the creative action which has unmade itself.

The *Odyssey* is unquestionably an extraordinary feat of endurance; it contains patches of evocative poetry; it makes one admire Kazantzakis' ability to organize and synthesize so much material on so many levels of signification. None of Kazantzakis' books represents his total doctrine so completely, none has more prophetic urgency, none is more devoted to the promulgation of his opinions. But is the *Odyssey* an achieved, successful work of art? Because a poem issues from its author's total vision does not mean that it is genuinely true to that vision, or able to evoke it for the reader. This is especially so in Kazantzakis' case, for his vision demanded its own annihilation. An absolutely conscious, willed fidelity, even to the third duty which systematized the system's overthrow, is a denial of the creative evolution on which Kazantzakis based his life. This is why I suggested that his total doctrine, though the crucial ingredient of everything he wrote, was also an obstacle in his path toward artistic perfection. To be genuinely true to himself, he had to develop a nonchalance and self-assurance enabling him to forget the system at least momentarily and to transubstantiate his urgent fidelity to it into an unmediated, naïve acceptance of life and death, a simple-minded awe.

This is precisely where the *Odyssey* fails. It is imperfect artistically because it is too faithful doctrinally, because we feel at every moment that the dynamo generating all 33,333 verses is the world-view and not an immediate feeling for human beings, human development, and human annihilation. I do not say that it fails because it is doctrinal poetry; rather that it does not do what its own doctrine expects of it.

In this poem Kazantzakis was too relentlessly the man-of-letters driving home his opinions. Distrustful of art's subtleties, he committed the technical mistakes of embodying the entire

[31]

evolutionary voyage in a single character and of being too relentlessly prophetic in his style. I must expand somewhat on these artistic problems, because they relate directly to Kazantzakis' growth in the years following the *Odyssey*. In a letter written while composing the epic, he claimed that he was "striving to experience the vanity of all endeavor and simultaneously the eternity of every moment." In Bergsonian terms this means that he was attempting to evoke (a) the Oneness which is the reality behind life's individuated shadows, and simultaneously (b) the paradox that only by believing these shadows to be real can we mount to a vision of their unreality. But the poem works against its own aims by placing the burden of both (a) and (b) on the single character of Odysseus. Though meant to interact with individual people and objects that are supposedly real, the over-universalized hero cannot do this convincingly because his own individuation is subordinated to his role as the life force's "succession without distinction," and also because he embodies Kazantzakis' solipsistic doctrine that the mind is the self-contained creative force out of which reality is spun. His object is to love all things and stick to none. But love presupposes a naïve belief in the reality of everyday life so that there may be relatedness between the lover and his beloved, so that the lover may both affect and be affected. Odysseus cannot have this naïve belief because he is Kazantzakis' totality; consequently he cannot relate either to people, history, or environment. He never allows himself to be touched in the fullest sense by someone else. Instead, he is an impervious, autonomous Self driving his way resolutely through experience like a wedge. In heaping every ingredient of universality upon Odysseus, Kazantzakis hoped to lead the reader beyond the individual to a sense of the All. What he accomplished, however, was merely to present the grotesquely magnified agonizing of a single alienated soul, and one who, precisely because of his

[32]

fabricated universality, never achieves the particularity which is the *sine qua non* of universal significance. Happily, Kazantzakis himself soon realized that one character cannot play a thousand different roles convincingly, that it is rather the author himself who must synthesize the contradictions and supply the unity, doing so surreptitiously while hiding in the wings. But this, in turn, demanded an artistic self-assurance which he at this point had not yet acquired.

The aim of conveying both a vision of Oneness and a sense of the eternity of every moment found further hindrance in Kazantzakis' style. As a poet, he achieved striking individual lines and a metaphorical richness unmatched in other writers, but never enough suppleness to evoke varying moods. We should compare his single verbal texture with the diversity seen in that other doctrinal epic, *Paradise Lost,* where the lushness of Eden, the undeniable grandeur of Satan, and the final serenity of our chastened first parents each dictates its appropriate rhythms and sonorities. Kazantzakis misses his goal of sublime urgency because his unvarying "high seriousness" weighs on the reader instead of uplifting him. Conversely, he fails to convey an unmediated sense of everyday life because his language never descends to quotidian simplicity. He did much better, fortunately, when he turned to prose.

These criticisms of the *Odyssey* should provide a way of discussing Kazantzakis' subsequent work because in certain of the later plays and novels the defects outlined above are at least partially remedied. In these works we feel the bull butting against the outward parts of Kazantzakis' totality; we apprehend a tension which provides artistic and human interest. Even if we decide ultimately that no one of the books can stand on its own as a masterpiece, we should recognize in the complete *œuvre* a very remarkable growth. The only enduring masterpiece, strangely, may be the entire career with its attempt to create a world-view and then its gradually developing need to transcend what it had created, without rejecting it.

The questions to ask in assessing Kazantzakis' growth should now be evident. For example: Does he create a thought-system and at the same time make us realize that absolute fidelity to that system is the system's ultimate denial? Does he truly fulfill his third duty—that is, fulfill it naïvely, without giving the feeling that it is consciously willed and thus still part of the intellectual system it is meant to transcend? Does he give us a genuine sense of the eternity of every moment, despite the abyss which ends existence? Does he develop a style sufficiently flexible to express the varying and contradictory moods which constitute his total experience? Does he convince us that his characters achieve a true relatedness with people and things outside them? Does he develop more sophisticated and subtle methods of synthesizing contradictions and pulling life's variety into oneness? Does he achieve universality without sacrificing particularity? Does he fuse history with cosmology and yet make us forget that his characters and incidents are formulaic?

Before attempting to see how these questions may be answered in relation to specific works written after the *Odyssey*, we should note three general factors which would seem to account for Kazantzakis' growth. These are: (1) his increasing reliance on prose, (2) his increasing sense of rootedness in Greece, and (3) his increasing acceptance of his own role as artist. By using prose, he liberated himself from the single texture to which verse restricted him. He was thus able to create linguistic embodiments for a much wider range of human moods and—if nothing else—to provide the variety which is the spice of art. By rooting himself once more in Greece (or rather, by *relaxing* sufficiently so that Greece's soil could embrace him, for rootedness demands humility and passive acceptance) he was

[34]

able to introduce into his works a natural, unforced, and therefore convincing particularity which they had hitherto lacked, a particularity which no amount of universalizing could then erase. Moreover, in helping him escape the tyranny of Mind and Self, this rootedness had the additional effect of allowing a true sense of community to an *oeuvre* which had tended formerly to individualism and indeed to solipsism. Lastly, by accepting his role as artist, he was able to draw from his worldview in a way that transcended it and thus paradoxically fulfilled its own prescriptions. Until this time, he had ostentatiously shielded himself against aestheticism, perhaps because he knew in his heart that his doctrine of the "abiding spirit" was if anything an aesthetic truth rather than a scientific one. When Kazantzakis came to accept as his innermost drive the normal artistic desire to cheat time by means of beauty, he gained a unity and peace he had lacked previously. This reconciliation with his own inescapable aestheticism enabled him to pay more attention to the technical side of his craft. It helped him to separate himself from his characters, to achieve an aesthetic distance, an aloofness arising not from indifference but from a calm engagement with the figures he alone had the power to immortalize. Much subdued now is the hysterical fervor of the early works in which his personal obsessions tended to vitiate the execution and which seemed determined to reform the world then and there, as though doubting their own longevity. Instead, in many (not all) of the later books we have a controlled fervor which presents us with Kazantzakis' own obsessions, to be sure, but at the same time dissolves these into the artistic whole. Because these works grow out of Kazantzakis' increased faith in art, they seem more willing to let art accomplish whatever improvements in our lives it is destined to accomplish, and in its own good time, in its own manner. In sum, by allowing his system to be aestheticized, Kazantzakis acquired the self-con-

[35]

fidence and nonchalance he needed if he was ever to escape the tyranny of Mind and consequently to fulfill his third duty in a genuine way.

All this came in fits and starts. Some of the works written after the *Odyssey* simply continue the old modes; in others the full range of growth is not always apparent. But scattered among certain of the novels and plays are unmistakable signs of change—all of which again makes it imperative for us to think of Kazantzakis' total career when we judge him.

A few examples will make this clearer. *Melissa*, though written shortly before the *Odyssey's* final draft, may be placed with the later works. (The epic was by this time in its definitive form except for minute verbal changes.) This play shows a remarkable advance in artistic control. Autobiographical elements are subordinated to internal artistic needs, ideas arise for the most part from the personalities of the characters who express them. At the same time, the play possesses earthiness and immediacy. In other words, Kazantzakis found a *mythos* which could effectively transubstantiate his own experiences into art, and handled that *mythos* with the dignified calm of a man who had faith in art's ability to speak to us on its own terms. As a result, the play does not strive baldly for sublimity by means of philological affectation and didactic importunity, as does the *Odyssey*. Its linguistic vehicle, prose, gives it a natural quality, exploiting the speech-rhythms and nonchalant fluency of demotic Greek. Yet this naturalness does not preclude an exalted and indeed epic flavor. What Kazantzakis began to do in this play was to achieve grandeur and prophetic urgency not by bulk or forced sublimity, but by simplicity. The most exalted moments are those in which humble everyday emotions are allowed to speak for themselves. Though, like all tragedy, the play attempts to show us the transitoriness of human life and a vision of something constant behind this transitoriness, it does this solely by

[36]

means of the particular. The characters are phantoms, yet they matter, they are real. We feel in *Melissa* the vanity of all endeavor and simultaneously the eternity of every moment.

The same elements of growth, as well as others, can be seen in the extraordinary play *Buddha*, which dates from 1941. Kazantzakis intended this work to be a *summa*, like the *Odyssey*. But it improves remarkably on the epic in its manner of handling a large amount of complicated and contradictory material. All possible human reactions are no longer squeezed unconvincingly into a single character. Those who respond actively and believe in the reality of phenomena are thus relieved of the subjectivism which constantly undermined Odysseus' credibility as a man in significant relation to the outside world. This subjectivism is now concentrated in the Magician and Poet who stand outside the drama proper, framing it in a much more artistically justifiable way than the rising and setting sun framed the epic. What Kazantzakis achieved here by means of more sophisticated craftsmanship was a successful wedding of realism and vision, of action and the knowledge that all action is futile. But craftsmanship is not alone responsible for this improvement. Another crucial factor is the aestheticizing of the play's subjectivity. Cosmological subjectivity remains, of course; there is still some non-object in the universe which is the energizing reality behind all these phantoms. Yet for practical purposes this energizing reality is now simply the artist. We are less aware that the characters are congealments of the life force, and more aware of something we find much easier to understand—that they are inventions of the artistic imagination. A wholly simple and familiar element of legitimate stylization is thus introduced into the play, for we grant the artist a right to make reality fit into a schema of his choosing, provided that he tricks us into forgetting both the schema and the ultimate control he exercises until he sees fit to remind us of them again. The excellence of

[37]

the result then depends on this exciting coexistence of artificiality and realism in a way that enhances both. This is achieved in *Buddha* and also, I believe, supremely in *Christ Recrucified* and *The Last Temptation.*

Zorba, written immediately after *Buddha,* is a crucial transition between that work and the later novels. In *Buddha,* the aesthetic attitude toward life is placed ostentatiously on a gangway between stage and audience; in *Zorba,* this attitude is much less visible, since it can be glimpsed only at the very end, peeking out through the wings. In *Christ Recrucified* and *The Last Temptation* it is completely hidden. These stages reflect Kazantzakis' increasing acceptance of phenomenal reality, an acceptance made possible, as I have said, by his progressive reconciliation both with Greece and with his own irrepressible aestheticism. *Zorba,* like everything Kazantzakis wrote, is a mythopoesis of Bergsonian doctrine, a parable showing the life force at work. Once more we see a creative action which unmakes itself. Human effort is shown to be futile and yet nonetheless radiant because people like Zorba, when they burn themselves out, imitate god, save him, push universal evolution toward the freedom of unencumbered spirituality. In this book, however, the cosmological element is subordinated to the artistic, indeed framed within it. At the very end we find as the "abyss" of spirituality neither the Silence of *Spiritual Exercises* nor the voiceless wail of the *Odyssey,* but Art. The book ends with the Boss sitting down and writing the book. All the events, all the transubstantiations, have conspired to enable the artistic flame within the Boss to be freed. He will now congeal his imagination into a *logos* and thereby save all the incidents and characters from oblivion.

This novel is a crucial fulcrum in Kazantzakis' career since it so openly records his passage from embroilment to serenity: the distanced noninvolvement of the artist. The events and

[38]

people the book records are Kazantzakis' own agonized tight-rope-dance between activism and Buddhistic withdrawal, his own journey by means of rationality, intuition, and action to the point where big ideas are transcended and he can truly say: "Where are we going? Do not ask!" This is the third duty, synthesizing life and death by means of the simple-minded, profound awe we see exemplified in that untutored yet quintessential artist, Zorba. In performing on the upper level of the icon what Zorba performs on the lower, the Boss accomplishes in action what Kazantzakis had envisioned in thought many years before. In his early career Kazantzakis had yearned for the freedom of perfect spirituality conceived first aesthetically, then in terms of Dionysian neo-paganism; this yearning was later "cosmologized" so that freedom became heroic cooperation with a universe that unmakes itself. The ideal figure was Odysseus, and Kazantzakis felt that he himself had attained the "Cretan glance" exemplified in his hero. "My own guide," he wrote in *Toda Raba* (1929), "is neither Faust nor Hamlet nor Don Quixote, but Don Odysseus." His meaning is clear from his glosses in a manuscript notebook. "Faust sought to find the essence behind appearances. Hamlet is entangled in appearances and writhes." Don Quixote gives way to a "ridiculous and sublime impetus." Odysseus "rejoices in appearances and, rejoicing, creates the essence." What Kazantzakis could not know at this time was that his definition of Odysseus was a perfect definition of the *artist* and that he himself would not achieve identification with his hero until he had re-aestheticized his cosmological yearnings to a significant degree and had thus become truer to his own impulses, bringing the Hamletian-Faustian-Quixotic transition more or less to an end. The novel *Zorba* records this transition and does so from the viewpoint of a man who had already achieved "Odyssean" freedom.

This is why the book succeeds. Because Kazantzakis himself

had already completed the growth depicted in the book, because he had attained a self-assurance enabling him to stand integrally in the wings viewing with equanimity his own agonized multiplicity, the book transcends its schematizations and dualities, embodying the synthesis it preaches. As in *Melissa,* a character is made to mouth the usual ideas about freedom. But in both works these ideas are felt to be more than hollow formulas since the works themselves now exemplify Kazantzakis' own liberation from the embroilments of his past.

In addition, they convey his thankfulness for everything that life offers. This loving and yet distanced relationship to his materials is carried forward in the final novels and especially in *Christ Recrucified* and *The Last Temptation.* (*Captain Michael, The Fratricides,* and *The Poor Man of God* strike me as flawed by comparison.) In the successful novels Kazantzakis' artistic self-assurance has reached the point where the energizing force can be kept entirely in the wings, invisible. The director is so confident now that he allows his characters to perform largely on their own. *Zorba,* despite obviously autobiographical content, transcends Kazantzakis' personality by establishing its characters as independent beings. *Christ Recrucified* carries this surpassing of the personal still further, for we now have a vivid evocation of community. Without in the least diminishing the importance or grandeur of its individual saviors of god, the novel convincingly demonstrates the individual's unreality apart from the oneness which is the group. This paradox is conveyed nonchalantly, without philosophical straining. As the refugees pick up their meagre belongings and set out once more despite the frustration they have just endured, we feel that, like the *élan vital* itself, they will continue to ascend higher and higher on the red track of earthly vicissitude, their collective impetus sweeping up courageous individuals as they go. What could have been just rhetoric (what indeed sounds like rhetoric here) is transformed by this book's simplicity into a successful evocation of both particularized human aspiration and the force which drives men to subordinate their personal well-being to a collective surge which will survive them.

Technically, *Christ Recrucified* and *The Last Temptation* walk a tightrope between stylization and realism, the universal and the particular. Insofar as Kazantzakis achieves a compelling evocation of real life, we are tricked into forgetting the rigidity of his schema; insofar as the schema calls up in us a compelling response in its own right, as happens especially in the two novels based on the Christ-story, we are tricked into forgetting the rigidity of plotting and characterization. Each element is a kind of sponge absorbing the defects of the other. Kazantzakis' ultimate accomplishment as a craftsman was the way he learned to exploit his limitations.

We return to the problem of criticism. Is Kazantzakis a universal genius, or the most overrated and atrocious writer of our times? Will his books be read fifty years from now or will they be completely forgotten once the present vogue runs out? I repeat that we cannot know. We can only know that he is widely appreciated today and that presumably he speaks to the condition of many people. He does this of course in the first instance through individual works, but the reason even a single, isolated book attracts us is because the totality of Kazantzakis' prophetic fervor, professionalism, and world-view is always discernible. When we dip more widely into his *oeuvre* we become alerted to the subtleties of that totality, and especially to the inward strains and tensions I have attempted to describe.

Those who read only sparingly will most likely find Kazantzakis appealing because of the opinions which he promulgated in everything he wrote—more accurately, because of the way he made these ideas incandescent. For some, the ideas themselves will seem less important than the sincerity and *élan* with which he voiced them. Others, however, will find that he speaks directly to their own needs. Like Kazantzakis, many people today are all too conscious that we have been born into a transitional age; like him, they crave an exit and feel that the direction must be away from materialism toward a new inwardness. Some people are already aware, as Kazantzakis was, that any such turn ought to be based on a comprehensive and hopefully scientific view of what life and death are all about; others are first awakened to this awareness by Kazantzakis. They share his strong determination to adjust the rhythm of individual behavior to a larger rhythm outside. They also appreciate his insistence that action, not withdrawal, is the way to spirituality, his equal insistence that action may take many forms, and his strict abhorrence of a linear, laissez-faire activism based on the gospel of increased gross national product. Like Kazantzakis, they wish to make the world better in concrete ways and they therefore value materiality; but at the same time their consciousness of the H-bomb makes them see how fragile materialistic progress can be and how right Kazantzakis was in his obsession with the dark abyss. Caught in Kazantzakis' own dilemma, they feel that his attempt to synthesize Western practicality and utopianism with an Eastern vision of universal vanity may give direction to their own gropings. On the other hand, many people are comforted by the way Kazantzakis seems unable to avoid Christianity and Hellenism when he bodies forth his visions of future man. His mixture of traditionalism and iconoclasm soothes at the same time that it disturbs.

These are some—certainly not all—of the reasons that Kazantzakis appeals today to so many thoughtful and searching people. But surely this is not enough to give him lasting value. Fifty years from now our present transitional age will presumably be over and our progeny will be caught in a different transition with different problems. If Kazantzakis is still read then, most likely it will be because of the basically human, and thus abiding, interest we find in him only when we know his *oeuvre* more or less as a whole. It is doubtful whether future generations will suddenly consider him a superb thinker or craftsman; they may, however, consider him a superb man. By this I naturally do not mean a perfect or even a good man but rather a superbly self-conscious one. Though Kazantzakis' great talent and drive perhaps never produced a book of the highest quality, they did produce a sprawling, undisciplined, impassioned *oeuvre* which gives us a remarkably intimate view of a living, straining totality, and in particular of an outward integument increasingly challenged by factors which enabled him to write better books than before but which by no means remade his entire being. It is the tensions in this contradictory yet integral totality that transform Kazantzakis from a pompous and stridently provincial rhetorician into a touchingly human figure worthy of our respect.

His autobiography, *Report to Greco*, holds a particular interest because it anthologizes and epitomizes the *oeuvre*, giving us a sense of the man in his wholeness. It shows us the busy man-of-letters promulgating his opinions while he races around the world and sends home dispatches to make a living; it allows the prophet to vent his sincerity and *élan*; it offers partial summaries of the world-theory. At the same time it attempts to aestheticize all these elements by giving the entire life an outward coherence it never possessed in reality, and it bears superb witness to Kazantzakis' eventual rootedness in things Greek and his awe-filled gratitude for the wonders of everyday life. The book thus tugs in different directions yet coheres in spite of itself because of the huge personality — the huge attempt at self-consciousness — which suffuses it.

The over-all witness Kazantzakis gave us is touching because beneath all its eclecticism and intellectual fireworks is a simple paradigm which has abiding validity. The first thing we see in him is the colossal intellectual arrogance of youth, the desire to control self and the world by understanding it. Next we see the clash in middle age between intellectual systems and a physical and psychological reality which refuses to be neatly contained within them. Finally, in old age, the youthful arrogance is confessed, surpassed to great degree, and yet not regretted. Kazantzakis acquires a serenity which is the distillation of everything that has gone before. It is a completely shaped life, a rebuke to the desultory, random lives of so many others, yet one whose validity comes only because the shaping forces were not wholly under Kazantzakis' own control. If everything had arisen from his own volition and foreknowledge, we would consider him an inhuman monster. The witness is a genuine one only because so many of the forces stood outside his desires and indeed warred against them. He gained serenity, one might say, in spite of himself; he honored his basically aesthetic instincts in spite of himself, still brandishing his prophetic fist. And though the arrogance decreased, the basic intellectual curiosity and the extraordinary articulateness did not. From beginning to end Kazantzakis tried to express what was happening to him, to understand (feelingly) even his own failure to understand. The result, as I have said, is a touching witness for self-consciousness, one which transcends self and becomes meaningful for all of us. If we think of Kazantzakis in his totality and see his individual books each as a different entrance to that living, straining wholeness, we shall appreciate how fully, notwithstanding his imperfect artistry, he performed the artist's primal task of giving a face to chaos.

SELECTED BIBLIOGRAPHY

NOTE: *Because Kazantzakis' manuscripts were often published erratically and after great delay, I list the works in the year they were writ-ten, in order to show their proper sequence. Conjectural dates of composition are followed by a question mark. N = novel, D = drama, T = travel articles, E = essay or article, Tr = translation, P = poetry, * indicates titles available in English. This list is far from complete. Those wishing fuller data should consult Katsimbalis' bibliography.*

Principal Works of Nikos Kazantzakis

1906	The Sickness of Our Age E
1906	Snake and Lily. N
1906	Day Is Breaking. D (produced 1907, never published)
1907–8	Letters from Paris. T
1908	Broken Souls. N (published serially, never in book form)
1908	Friedrich Nietzsche's Philosophy of Law and the State. E
1909	The Masterbuilder. D
1909?	Comedy. D
1909	The Demoticists' Society "Solomos" of Irakleion, Crete. E
1910–15	(Translations of works by Darwin, Nietzsche, Bergson, etc.)
1912?	H. Bergson. E
1915?	Nikephoros Phokas. D
1915?	Odysseas. D
1915?	Christ. D (This play, and the two preceding, were re-worked at various times in the 1920s.)
1920–24	(Letters, in:) Letters to Galateia. Athens, 1958.
1923	*Spiritual Exercises. E (= Saviors of God)
1924	Odyssey, first draft of books 1–6. P
1924–25?	Confession of Faith. E (missing in Katsimbalis; published in *Nea Ephēmeris,* Irakleion, February 26, 1925)
1925	(Travel articles on Russia)
1926	(Travel articles on Palestine, Cyprus, Spain)
1927	(Travel articles on Italy, Egypt, Sinai)
1927	Rosa Luxemburg. E
1927	Odyssey, first draft of books 7–24. P
1927	Impressions of Soviet Russia. T
1928	(Revision of Spiritual Exercises)
1928	"What Is Happening in Russia." (speech; published in *Anagennēsē,* Athens, January, 1928, pp. 193–98)

1929	*Toda Raba. N (written in French)
1929	Odyssey, second draft. P
1930	History of Russian Literature. E
1930–31	(Children's books; one half of a French-Greek dictionary)
1930–31?	(Expanded version of "Confession of Faith"; translation published in Helen Kazantzakis, pp. 565–70)
1932	Dante, Divine Comedy. Tr
1932–37	Terzinas. P (published in a collected edition, Athens, 1960)
1933	*Spain 1933. T
1933	Contemporary Spanish Lyrical Poetry. Tr
1935	*(Travel articles on Japan and China)
1936	*Le Jardin des Rochers. N (= The Rock Garden)
1936	Pirandello, Questa Sera Si Recita a Soggetto. Tr
1936	Goethe, Faust, Part One. Tr
1936	Fear and Hunger. E (reprinted in Vrettakos, pp. 577-79)
1936	*What I Saw for 40 Days in Spain. T
1937	Othello Returns. D
1937	*Contemporary Greece: Journey to the Morea. T
1937	*Melissa. D
1938	*Odyssey, seventh and last draft. P
1939	Julian the Apostate. D
1940	*(Travel articles on England)
1941	Buddha. D (second draft, 1943)
1941	*Life and Times of Alexis Zorbas. N (second draft, 1943) (= Zorba the Greek)
1942	Homer, Iliad. Tr (with Prof. I. Th. Kakridis)
1943	Prometheus the Fire-bringer; Prometheus Bound; Prometheus Unbound. D (trilogy)
1943	Jens Johannes Jörgensen, Saint Francis. Tr
1943–44	Homer, Odyssey. Tr (with Prof. I. Th. Kakridis; reworked 1956–57)
1944	Kapodistrias. D
1944	Constantine Palaiologos. D
1948	Sodom and Gomorrah. D
1948	*Christ Recrucified. N (= The Greek Passion)
1949	*Fratricides. N (second draft, 1954)
1949	*Kouros. D
1949	*Christopher Columbus. D
1949–50	*Captain Michael. N (= Freedom or Death)
1950–51	*The Last Temptation. N

[46]

1953   *The Poor Man of God.   N   (= Saint Francis)
1955–56   *Report to Greco (autobiography)

1902–57   *(Letters and other documents, in:) Helen Kazantzakis,
            Nikos Kazantzakis. New York, 1968.
1926–57   (Letters and other documents, in:) Four Hundred Letters
            of Kazantzakis to Prevelakis. Athens, 1965.

Secondary Sources

Alexiou, Ellē. Gia na ginei megalos. Athens, 1966.

Anapliotis, J. The Real Zorba and Nikos Kazantzakis. Chicago, 1968.

Anthonakes, Michael A. "Christ, Freedom and Kazantzakis." Unpublished dissertation, New York University, 1966.

Bien, Peter. Kazantzakis and the Linguistic Revolution in Greek Literature. Princeton, 1972.

——"Kazantzakis and Politics," in George A. Panichas, ed., The Politics of Twentieth-Century Novelists. New York, 1971.

——"Kazantzakis' Nietzschianism," Journal of Modern Literature, Winter, 1971–72.

——"Zorba the Greek, Nietzsche, and the Perennial Greek Predicament," Antioch Review, Spring, 1965, pp. 147–63.

Dillistone, F. W. The Novelist and the Passion Story. London, 1960.

Doulis, Tom. "Kazantzakis and the Meaning of Suffering," Northwest Review, Winter, 1963, pp. 33–57.

Friar, Kimon. "Introduction," in Nikos Kazantzakis, The Odyssey. New York, 1958.

——"Introduction," in Nikos Kazantzakis, The Saviors of God—Spiritual Exercises. New York, 1960.

Hoffman, Frederic J. The Imagination's New Beginnings: Theology and Modern Literature. Notre Dame, 1968.

Izzet, Aziz. Nikos Kazantzaki: Biographie. Paris, 1965.

Janiaud-Lust, Colette. Nikos Kazantzaki: Sa vie, son œuvre, 1883–1957. Paris, 1970.

Journal of Modern Literature (Philadelphia), Winter, 1971–72. (Issue devoted to Kazantzakis.)

Jouvenel, Renaud de. "En Souvenir de Kazantzaki," Europe, June, 1958, pp. 85–105.

Kainouria Epochē (Athens), Autumn, 1958. (Issue devoted to Kazantzakis.)

Katsimpalēs, G. K. Bibliographia N. Kazantzakē Á 1906–1948. Athens, 1958.

Kazantzakis, Helen. Nikos Kazantzakis. New York, 1968.

Nea Estia (Athens), Christmas, 1959. (Issue devoted to Kazantzakis.)

Nea Estia (Athens), Christmas, 1971. (Issue devoted to Kazantzakis.)

Parker, Sandra A. "Kazantzakis in America: A Bibliography of Translations and Comment," *Bulletin of Bibliography,* XXV (1968), 166–70.

Prevelakis, Pandelis. Nikos Kazantzakis and His Odyssey. New York, 1961.

——"Nikos Kazantzakēs, symbolē stē chronographia tou biou tou," *Nea Estia,* Christmas, 1959. (French translation in Izzet.)

——"Schediasma esoterikēs biographias," in Tetrakosia grammata tou Kazantzakē ston Prebelakē. Athens, 1965.

Rooke, Rodney J. "Nikos Kazantzakis, a Bibliography." Unpublished thesis, University of London, August, 1965.

Stanford, W. B. The Ulysses Theme. Oxford, 1954.

Vrettakos, Nikēphoros. Nikos Kazantzakēs: Ē agonia tou kai to ergo tou. Athens, n.d. [1957].

Zōgraphou, Lilē. N. Kazantzakēs: Enas tragikos. Athens, 1960.

Columbia Essays on Modern Writers

Editor: William York Tindall
Advisory Editors: Jacques Barzun, W. T. H. Jackson, Joseph A. Mazzeo